Gifts

poetry that reaches your heart

Jenna Plewes

ISBN-13978-1495394409

To all those people who opened my eyes and my heart to the beauty of the world and led me to God.

Acknowledgements

Some of these poems have appeared in Areopagus, The Dawntreader, Reach, Poetry Cornwall, and First Time magazines

Contents

'Patches of God, light in the woods of our experience'

C S Lewis

Taize

A needle of light in the weave
drawing a thread
through silence,
stitching a prayer.

Compline

Centuries kneel beside his effigy
head pillowed on stone
eyes fixed on eternity

an endless murmur of prayer
drifts round his tomb
rises like warm breath to the fronded roof

compline, sung each night
when work is done,
unties the days concerns

and monks and nuns
slip gently into sleep
murmuring compline in their beds.

—

Open-eyed Prayer

The soil is sliding into sleep
smelling of sun and heat
stored and swaddled
safe for spring,
I stand among the bean poles
falling sideways now
sticks and vine stalks
tangling courgette plants,
their leaves crisp as toast.

A shadow moves across the field
a breeze ruffles the grass,
a wash of sunshine
touches the wind spinners
copper and steel catch the light
spiderlings float past
on threads tenuous as hope.

—

Silence

The silence of the early dawn
wrapped in skeins of mist
enfolds your peace
the silence of a little church
whitewashed and spare
enfolds your peace

the silence of a lonely valley
at the end of a long and stony climb
enfolds your peace
the silence of a quiet night
and a diamond- studded sky
enfolds your peace

silence that smooths out the wrinkles of care,
that untangles the knots of fear and pain
and loosens the tight grip on control
silence that slows our racing feet
and reaches deep into our souls
silence that brings with it calm,

that calm in which I hear your voice.

Legacy

The Romans built straight roads
held the high ground
took no detours
saw alien eyes hostile
hidden places traps.

Holy men like meandering streams
sought the easiest route
skirting the rocks
 and boggy ground
embracing the unexpected
finding men good.

Celtic saint and consul
each left their mark
statute and law
order and control
dreams ,visions and song
glimpses of immortality
all woven into the fabric of this land.

The Map of Cornish Saints in Truro Cathedral

Fireflies scatter coast and cliff and moor
hundreds of churches

founded by men who walked the lanes
sandalled and weatherbeaten

lacing our wind-scoured land
in psalms and prayers

tying a rope of faith to each grey church
each lichen-crusted cross.

Headlights blind the busy roads
ricochet stop signs, warnings, traffic cones

but in deep lanes on quiet nights
the rope still holds.

Stork

A slender silhouette
from a Japanese print
she stands on a crown of twigs
guarding her young

outstaring the sun and moon
the ceaseless conversation
of the surf
the turning tides

her universe a pinnacle of rock
far from the convoluted working of the world
narrowed to a single thought

a state of grace
that slips like sunlight into each soul

for a few seconds.

Effigies of a lord and his lady

Side by side they lie in stony silence
anger burnt to ashes
love leeched long ago

sunset quickens the stained glass
jewels a pillar, a flagstone
warms the tomb

for a moment it seems his hand moves
their fingers meet,
she blushes, her lips tremble,

while outside the sun-baked gravestones
cool
the light dies.

The Unlocking

You took my hand
placed it just so
I felt
sliding between my fingers
something alive
that slid free
you wrote 'water'
in my palm.

You took my face
between your hands,
bent it
gently down,
I breathed something sweet
like a soft kiss
you wrote 'blossom',
placed the petals
in my hand.

I have them still
paper thin,
precious.

Midwinter Murmuration

The longest night is coming
the sea shivers

in the thin light millions of starlings
wheel and turn like a shoal of fish

become a turbaned genie
rising from the dunes

a twist of smoke, a snake, a raised fist
millions of desires welded into one

an orchestra of voices
holding a single note for a breathing space

till with a long sigh they fall like charred fragments
rasping the reed bed.

Midwinter Moon

Caught in midwinter branches
a fingernail paring
bright in the blue black night
so fragile it might snap, like ice
that films the ruts in the lane
skeletal trees net the stars
on this the longest night of the year.

Christmas Eve

Snow came after dark tonight
holding its breath
swaddled the sleeping town
hushed the familiar streets
our steps were the first steps
as we walked home
on this, the holiest night of the year.

New year's Eve

The top of the hill touches the stars
sways in the darkness
far below, the village gleams
awake and singing
bright flowers bloom in the dark
music tangles the breeze
on this, the final night of the year.

So Simple,

all the creator's love
held in a trusting girl

while stars blaze
and every pebble sings.

At Christmas

You came a tiny baby
defenceless--- you defend us

you came unknown, and poor
homeless----you are our home

you came to us with empty hands
to give us everything

you emptied out yourself
to fill our emptiness

you put on our humanity
to show us how to live

You chose to die for us
so we could be with you
always.

See the Child

Go and see
don't try to understand

stoop under the wooden lintel
kneel by the crib
on the hard packed earth

see in the lamplight
long dark lashes
tiny fingernails

in the shadows and the warmth
hear the bleating of a lamb
the rustle of straw

through the still small hours
listen to the soft breathing of a baby.

The Meaning of Christmas

A teenage mother in a mucky shed
laboured to birth him

no midwife, no pretty baby clothes
ready to greet him

no happy news to family and friends
waiting to celebrate.

A fugitive from an occupied land
changed our perceptions

a great ruler was ignored
but shepherds were told

angels sang in the heavens
and wise men knelt

the meek shall inherit the earth
at the end of time

our world will be turned upside down
only love will remain.

Mary's tale

It all began in a stable
far from home

heavy with God's son
I waited till the long night ended
the baby cried

it ended on a rubbish dump
far from home

heart-broken for my son
I waited as the long day throbbed with pain
he cried, just once, he died

it was a long road
helplessness and fear walked with me
love held my hand

a thrush sang in the early morning light
I heard my name.

Maundy Thursday Service, Washing of feet

Stepping softly from sensible shoes
toes shrinking from cold stone
she waits her turn

ice cold sea
skirt tucked high
sun splintering shallows

feet cradled in huge hands
warm water on cracked skin, blotted with gentleness
pricking of unexpected tears

Salt sticky skin,
sandpapered dry
gritty sandals, shifting shingle

Just once a year
the feel of fingers
pressing love in every thirsty pore.

The Pieta by Michaelanglo

She sits gowned in grief
gently letting go of him
giving him back

unseen, beyond all pain
the pulse of God is gathering itself
to burst the crust of death
and set us free.

Easter

Some time in the night
in the long hours of darkness
the binding, winding sheets emptied
dawn slid back the stone
he strode into sunlight

and those whose pillows were wet with grief
dragged themselves from their beds
to find everything changed
and little by little it dawned on them
that they too could be free.

Joseph

a quiet man
a man who listened, kept his word
married his girl
pregnant, and not by him the rumour went

lived abroad for several years
came home with a teenage son
taught him how to work with wood
missed him when he left

watched his son become a man
a man he didn't understand
a man they called 'the son of man'
and loaded with their dreams

died before it all went wrong
was spared the pain of standing by
seeing his son go to his death
without a fight.

Mary saw the sun rise
saw it shine into the empty tomb
went home alone
stood in the empty kitchen
told him the news.

The kingdom

The world is full of voices
crying and criticizing
complaining and cajoling
laughing and lamenting
looking for answers that satisfy
and finding none,

but His is a kingdom of silence
where all questions have been answered
and no more words need to be said
then deep within us we shall feel
the slow soft breathing of the universe
and in that stillness hear the voice of God.

Second Coming

I've been expecting Him
he didn't say when
he said watch for me
but no time or date
I was never sure
but I hoped
I hoped He'd come.

I expected a big parade
an army of saints
sun glinting off breastplates
trumpets blaring, cheering crowds
a big parade you couldn't miss.

The picture I have now
is very different
He'll come in love
in the mighty power of love
He'll come surrounded by children
there'll be laughter and singing
and lots of hugs and smiles
there'll be tears of repentance
there'll be tears of joy
there'll be the end of things
as we know them
but it won't be the end
it will be the beginning.

Exhibition of Christian Art

Puritan monotone
amidst golden alleluias,
one picture dominates the room

a solitary tree
like the outline of fingers
on a fogged window

when you look closer
infinite gradations of grey
wash across the canvas

suddenly you see
a cone of opalescence
spreads from a core of white

and you move through the paint
into the silence and stillness of dawn
towards a blaze of light from the empty tomb.

Gifts

You gave me my own song
entrusted me to sing my tune
if I refuse the music will be lost.

You gave me my own voice
entrusted only me to speak my words
if I am silent they will not be heard.

You gave me my own work
entrusted me to do my tasks
if I neglect them they will not be done.

You gave me my own gifts
entrusted only me with their fulfilling
if I refuse, their beauty will be lost

so help me find my song, and sing with joy
help me use my voice, and speak with love
help me know my work and use my gifts
my life, my love to worship you.

'Every Particle of You and Me was Forged in the Furnaces of Space'

Tell me God
did you swirl stillness like wine in a glass
circle its rim with your wetted forefinger
setting space singing

did you fling back the shuttered dark
set fire to a zillion suns
wrap the body of a new-born world
in a blanket of light

did you breathe a white-fire heat
meld matter and flux
pour life's metal in a myriad of molds
to cool in the winds of time

Did you spin a silken web of love
and tangle all our lives within the threads
that thrill with every sob and every smile
and resonate,
              and resonate,
                        and resonate?

—

Unknowable God

Can a man mold the wind with his fingers
or hold back the tide with his hands
can he visit the soul of another
and stand where another soul stands?

He may learn to explore and examine
the intricate web that life weaves
but mystery clouds his perceptions
and doubt surrounds all he achieves

can a raindrop envisage the ocean,
an acorn acknowledge the tree
a pebble remember the mountain
a wave know it's part of the sea?

We believe we can master creation
make a partisan God be our friend
but eternity snuffs out our hubris
awestruck we kneel at the end

yet love underpins our existence
and peace comes unbidden in prayer
beauty still gilds the horizon
and goodness is found everywhere

we scrabble to find ourselves answers,
we search for a definite proof,
but the wonder of our becoming
        is all we can grasp of the truth.

—

The Milky Way

The ash of a zillion worlds
drifts overhead

shooting stars
harrow the darkness

thoughts blunder like moths
in the listening place.

"Life is a narrow bridge"

Given a sack to put a lifetime in
I carried simple things at first

sunlight on a fat green leaf
a raindrop in a spider's web

I added skipping songs and fairytales
and then I put in heavier things

love affairs and existential thoughts
I found it stretched and added work

marriage, and motherhood and care
it filled up too with grief and loss

heavy with the fear of failure
the need to please, the 'oughts' and 'shoulds'

they took the space I wanted for delight
for freedom to explore and take a risk

the room to laugh and be at peace
to love my neighbour and to love my God

I need to empty out the heaviness
learn to travel as a child again

on the narrow bridge across the abyss
as it sways in the wind.

34

———

These are the Places

There are some places where the membrane's thin
where life is governed by unworldly laws,
preoccupations fade, new dreams begin.

Sometimes a smell from childhood draws you in,
a tune you had forgotten makes you pause
there are some places where the membrane's thin.

The trophies that you tried so hard to win
look tarnished here, you notice all the flaws,
preoccupations fade, new dreams begin.

Some search for many years to find within
themselves a peace the world ignores,
there are some places where the membrane's thin;

a quiet church, high vaulted, cool and dim
where joy and pain soak into ancient walls,
preoccupations fade, new dreams begin;

calm seas and hills where breezes brush your skin
the lonely places where your spirit soars
these are the places where the membrane's thin
preoccupations fade, new dreams begin.

Stilled

The sea was a lake of milk
no ripples, no waves, no sound
above us stretched a sheet of cloud
woven without a seam or break
no sun or stars to pinpoint our position

we saw no land
no weed, no rock, no floating thing
we left no wake,
no trace of where we'd been
our oars dipped and rose
the water opened for us
closed behind
we had no measure of how far we moved
or if we moved at all

maybe the water moved and
we were chained to
something
buried so deep beneath the skin
we would never know
its shape
its weight

we dipped our oars
watched water drop from the blades
we went on breathing in and out
while fathoms deep
something held

Leave Me in the Light

When I die
don't put me underground
cut down a giant oak
as they did
four thousand years ago

pull out the stump
drag it across the wide salt marsh
with honeysuckle ropes
upend it where the curlews call

lay me across its outstretched hand
under the sun, the moon
the turning stars

encircle me in
fifty trunks of oak
each split in two
fold a seamless skin of bark around my bier

leave me the smell of fresh cut wood
the shine of pale oak flesh
the sound of wind and tide

birds will clean my bones
midsummer's rising sun will
find me through the keyhole of the east
and when midwinter sunrise looks for me
I will be gone.

The End is a Beginning

an endless spiral
upwards and upwards
on the thermals
of God's love,
a tiny speck
circling
in the blue
 of eternity.
Out of sight
of human eyes
but in full view
of Him,
safely held
in His eternal
freedom.

29503444R00025

Made in the USA
Charleston, SC
14 May 2014